THE CATHOLIC CHURCH IN BOSTON

Published on 14th October 1977, to mark the

150th Anniversary

of the foundation of

SAINT MARY'S CHURCH
BOSTON

1827 — 1977

History of Boston Series

This series is designed to consist of individual papers and material relevant to the history of the town of Boston in the county of Lincolnshire in England. These papers – which may be short and published several to a booklet or long enough to justify booklets to themselves – will range widely over many aspects of the life of the town. Some indeed may deal mainly with people and events far removed from Boston, but only in so far as they have a relevance to the history of the town itself.

All the papers in this series will be contributed by individuals through the 'History of Boston Project', usually from the material that they will have accumulated towards the proposed eventual book *The History of Boston*. However, although all papers are the work of the individual authors, who retain full responsibility for their own contributions, every paper (other than reprints from the documents of history themselves) is submitted to a professional authority before acceptance. Whether or not the professional advice is accepted is the responsibility of the individual author but nothing will be published in this series which is thought to be historically inaccurate or in any other way unacceptable as a work of history.

Consultant Emeritus in Local History to the History of Boston Project

Alan Rogers, M.A., Ph.D., F.R.Hist.S., F.S.A., Senior Lecturer in Medieval and Local History, Department of Adult Education, University of Nottingham. Editor of *Bulletin of Local History East Midlands Region.* Edited *The Making of Stamford* (1965); *Stability and Change : some aspects of N. and S. Rauceby in the Nineteenth Century* (1969). Author of *The Medieval Buildings of Stamford* (1970), *A History of Lincolnshire* (1970), *This Was Their World* (1972), and of several papers on aspects of Lincolnshire history. Chairman of the History of Lincolnshire Committee.

History of Boston Series — Number Fifteen   ISSN 0305-2079

THE CATHOLIC CHURCH

IN

BOSTON

by

MARTIN MIDDLEBROOK

Published for the History of Boston Project jointly with
the Parish of St. Mary's, Boston

RICHARD KAY PUBLICATIONS

80 Sleaford Road, Boston, Lincolnshire, PE21 8EU

1977

The Author

Martin Middlebrook was born in Boston in 1932 and has been a parishioner of Saint Mary's all his life except when absent from the town for the latter part of his education or on National Service. His early education was at Saint Mary's Catholic School. He once attended a junior seminary to train as a missionary priest but left because he felt that he did not have a vocation for that life.

He has been involved in the public life of Boston since 1958 and in 1966 he became the youngest ever Mayor of the town.

He began his career as an author with the publication in 1971 (after three years of research and writing) of *The First Day on the Somme*, the first of his 'Men at War' trilogy. The details of his other books appear inside the front cover and their sales already exceed 100,000 copies. His work has been translated into German and his books published in Britain, U.S.A., and Germany. He wrote *Boston at War* which appeared as the twelfth publication in the History of Boston Series.

Acknowledgements

We are grateful to The Revd. Dr. Kenneth W. Stevenson for having read the original typescript and for his helpful comments thereon.

The illustrations have been provided from many sources and it is not possible to identify the orgins of all. We are however grateful to Addy's of Boston for permission to reproduce *Figs* 10, 13, 20, and to the *Lincolnshire Standard* for *Fig* 17.

The publisher wishes particularly to acknowledge the very great co-operation afforded by the staff of the Guardian Press without which this booklet could not have been produced in time for the Saint Mary's 150th anniversary celebrations.

CONTENTS

ILLUSTRATIONS

INTRODUCTION

In 1827 a new Catholic church was built in Horncastle Road, Boston. It was dedicated to Saint Mary the mother of Jesus Christ, and several generations of Catholics have worshipped there since that date. Now, 150 years later, I have been asked to write a short history to commemorate this important event. Because Catholics regard the Christian religion that existed up to the Reformation as the original Catholic Faith, this account is not confined to the last 150 years. Although I do not wish to be controversial, it must be stated that, for Catholics, the building of a new church in 1827 was not the establishment of a new form of religion but the re-establishment in this town of their original faith.

Unfortunately, the discovery that Saint Mary's was in its 150th Anniversary year was not made until the year had more than half passed. It was decided to hold a celebration in October of the year and I was asked to produce this booklet by that month. Because of this, I have had to carry out this work without the period of leisurely research that I would have liked and most of my work was done at a time when both the parish priest and Sister Hilda, the long-serving head teacher of the primary school, were away on holiday. Another drawback has been the shortage of material from the early years, before living memory. Nevertheless, I am satisfied that there are no serious gaps in the events described but if any reader feels that I have omitted minor events that should have been included I hope that he or she will make allowance for the rushed conditions under which I have worked. As well as marking the 150th Anniversary of St Mary's Church this booklet is also appearing as the 15th publication in the History of Boston Series. I hope that non-Catholic readers will excuse my occasional 'parochial' sentiment.

A large share of the credit for the material researched for the booklet, and presented here, should go to the splendid response from several people who were approached for help with various aspects of research. My sincere thanks are due to Canon Martin Cumming of Nottingham Cathedral, Father Francis Edwards S. J. of Farm Street, London, Father C. H. O'Brien of Oldcotes, Canon G. D. Sweeney of Loughborough and, in Boston, to Sister Hilda and to several of the parishioners of Saint Mary's. For documentary research, I have consulted Pishey Thompson's *History of Boston*, Canon A. M. Cook's *Boston*, George Jebb's *Church of Saint Botolph* and the Catholic Truth Society's handbook *Martyrs of England and Wales* 1535–1680.

Finally, let me say that I may not be the wholly detached and impartial chronicler of events that I should be. I was born in this parish; I was baptized and married in Saint Mary's church and have also seen my own daughters baptized there.

To the twenty two parish priests who have ministered
to the Catholics of Boston during
the past 150 years.

BEFORE

THE PARISH OF SAINT MARY

THE FIRST COMING OF THE CHURCH

Legend has it that the Christian religion came to Boston before there was even a town here. A good and holy Saxon gentleman, Botolph, born early in the Seventh Century, decided in about his fortieth year to retire from his life of study and commerce and he obtained permission from King Ethelmund of East Anglia to establish a monastery. The legend says that the site chosen by Botolph was an isolated place near the mouth of the River Witham on a piece of higher ground among the surrounding fens just upstream from the established settlement of Skirbeck. The place where the monastery was built is supposed to have been called Icanhoe, meaning 'ox Island'. The monastery built at Icanhoe was probably no more than a collection of small wooden buildings. Botolph and his monks lived peacefully here until his death about the year 680. The saintly monk was later canonized and 17th June is recognized as his feast day. The community of monks that he had established lasted until 870 when all the wooden buildings were burnt in a Danish invasion. But a few private dwellings had probably remained around the monastery site and these and a small chapel remained after the monks had been driven out. This settlement was supposed to have been the first Boston – 'Botolph's Town'.

Unfortunately the above account may be no more than legend as far as Boston is concerned. There is now stronger evidence that Saint Botolph's monastery at 'Icanhoe' was in Suffolk and that he may never have even visited the area where Boston now stands. The first origins of Boston and the circumstances in which Christianity came to the town are now lost in the mists of time. Boston may have no stronger link with Botolph than to have been named after a holy man whose reputation had spread from Suffolk.

The coming of the Normans after 1066 revitalized Christianity in England but Boston remained only a tiny place in the shadow of the more important Skirbeck until a new bridge was built at Boston in, or just before, 1305. (The present 'old Town Bridge', near the Market Place, is on or near the 1305 bridge and is the third one on that site.) This new bridge, being the lowest bridging point on the Witham was the signal for Boston's growth. The town prospered and Christianty and the religious institutions of the period thrived with it. The next 200 years saw the establishment of a peak of religious activity in Boston. The centrepiece of this was, of course, the tall parish church of Saint Botolph, often known now as 'The Stump'. The building of this was started in 1309 on the site of a smaller stone church. It took approximately 150 years for this great

9

new church to be completed and, at its busiest period just before the Reformation, the total number of priests at Saint Botolph's may have been as high as thirty-nine.

Monastic religious life also became established in Boston although the town never had one of the abbeys, whose influential abbots wielded such power in those years; the nearest abbey was at Swineshead. There were three friaries belonging to the Grey, Black (or Dominican), and Augustinian orders; a Benedectine priory, and a small convent, probably dedicated to Saint Anne. Most commercial life was also integrated into the church and among the powerful Guilds in Boston were those of the Holy Trinity, Corpus Christi, the Blessed Mary, and Saint Peter.

One of the institutions of that period which may be of particular interest to today's Catholics was a hospital, established about the year 1200, for poor people and dedicated at first to Saint Leonard. This was situated near what is now known as Hospital Lane, probably where there is now the small group of old people's bungalows in St Leonard's Close. It was soon taken over by the Knights Hospitallers of Saint John of Jerusalem who renamed the hospital after their patron saint. This institution, which had its own chapel and clergy, existed for about 400 years and it is a happy thought for present-day Catholics that their own church is so close to the site of that earlier institution with it long history of pious and charitable work.

THE REFORMATION AND THE PILGRIMAGE OF GRACE

The end of this era came in the 1530s. The Christian Church had changed much in those years and it must be admitted that many of its activities, from those of the Pope in Rome, right down through the hierarchy, had drifted from the simple Christianty of Saint Peter, the first Pope, and his early church. A cleansing from within might have held the Church together and Christians in Boston would perhaps still be worshipping under the same roof. Instead, the Popes did nothing and the reforming zeal came from without, from men whom the Popes called heretics. A great 'protesting' movement spread from the mainland of Europe to England. King Henry VIII, who wanted to be rid of his first wife, Catherine of Aragon, used this new movement first to challenge the Pope and then to defy him completely and establish himself as the only head of the Christian Church in this country. The 'Anglican' religion thus became the 'established' religion and in this way came to Boston.

This was not a new religion but merely another form of Christian worship, the main aspect of which was a complete denial of the Pope as head of the Church. It is understandable that some sort of reform was long overdue but the new order was imposed with an intolerance and later with a savagery that was decidedly un-Christian. This was perhaps because allegiance to the Roman Catholic Church meant allegiance to the Pope, which by implication meant opposition to the king, and this could be regarded as treason.

Like many smaller monasteries all over the country, the three friaries and, probably, the Benedictine priory in Boston were closed and the friars turned out to join thousands of their brothers tramping the roads of England as destitute beggars. The ordinary clergy were given a simple choice – acknowledge the King as head of their church or be classed as traitors with a good chance of being put to death. Led by their bishops, the vast majority of the English clergy repudiated Rome and the 'Church of England' carried on in the same churches that the Roman Church had used for several centuries. There is no record that at that time the Boston priests showed any serious opposition to the new form of religion although some may have quietly resigned their livings. The later dissensions in the Anglican Church are not a part of this story and must be sought elsewhere.*

The ordinary townspeople, however, were not satisfied. They had long been used to hearing Mass in Latin, which the Anglicans gave up, the poor had often benefitted from the friars in the town, and there were rumours that many new taxes were about to be levied in the name of the new religion. A rebellion started at Louth and groups of men from many parts of the county started to march on Lincoln and challenge the King's assumption of control over their old religion. The degree of support for this movement must have varied from place to place and for many reasons. A party from Boston and the surrounding villages, possibly as many as 2,000 men, joined this movement but what the history books later called the Pilgrimage of Grace soon faded away without having made any contact with the King's forces, and the would-be rebels drifted back to their homes. King Henry was determined to exact some punishment however. Lord Hussey, the Boston nobleman, had tried hard not to become involved with the popular rising but was executed nevertheless and several other Boston men were also among the 100 Lincolnshire men put to death. These men may be classed as among the first in a long line of English martyrs. There were no more recorded protests in Boston against the new form of religion. The Church of England became the only form of worship allowed and a rigorous prohibition of the old Roman religion was imposed. There was a brief relaxation of this for five years when Queen Mary, daughter of Henry VIII and Catherine of Aragon, ruled from 1553 to 1558 but she was just as savage in her persecution of the Protestants. Elizabeth I came to the throne on Mary's death and resumed the ways of Henry VIII and, for the next 250 years, the Roman Catholic Church in any organized form disappeared from the town of Boston.

---

* Some details of religious dissension in later centuries in Boston can be found in earlier History of Boston publications – see particularly H. of B. No. V *The Puritan Town of Boston* by Mark Spurrell and H. of B. No. VI *Methodism in Boston* by William Leary.

PENAL TIMES

These sad years were known as the Penal Times and for 140 of those years it required the utmost faith and courage to be a Roman Catholic. It was high treason to practise the Catholic religion and to hold that the Pope was still head of the Christian Church. One could be required to swear an oath of allegiance to Queen Elizabeth and her successors, acknowledging them as supreme in spiritual matters. To stamp out the Roman religion, a relentless hunt for priests and those laymen who gave shelter to the priests took place during those years. If the priests could be stamped out, the religion would die. But, after the Catholic seminaries in England had been closed down, a steady stream of new priests continued to arrive in the country. Most of these came from the seminary at Douai in France. This college was founded by a group of exiled Oxford academics and priests, headed by Cardinal William Allen. Douai became almost a 'Catholic Oxford in exile' and Cardinal Allen was appointed by the Pope to be head of the English Church in exile; the Pope also financed the college. Douai produced more than 300 English-born priests during the first thirty penal years and 160 of these died for their faith. Six years after the first Douai priests arrived in England, they were joined by a much smaller force of English Jesuit priests sent direct from Rome. These 'recusant' priests had to enter the country secretly, conceal their profession, and say Mass only in secret. They were hunted down by the authorities with great intensity. £100, a large amount of money in those days, was the reward to an informer. A great many of these brave priests were discovered and arrested. They were then challenged to renounce the Pope and acknowledge the reigning King or Queen as head of the Church. Most were tortured to persuade them to do this. Some priests were then exiled but most were condemmed to death. Their martyrdom took the most cruel form – to be hanged, drawn, and quartered in public was the usual sentence for 'Popish' priests. The 'drawing', or cutting out of the heart and other internal organs, was often commenced while the poor priest was still living. The 'quartering', or cutting of the body into four parts, was followed by public exhibition of those parts for several days. The same treatment, or sometimes a more simple hanging, was the fate also of many laymen caught sheltering priests in their homes.

The harassed priests could not cover the whole country. They travelled from one safe house to another, mostly in the cities or in those country areas where loyal landowners kept the Catholic faith alive. No priests are known to have been caught at Boston and it is probable that none ever ministered here. A record exists of a letter sent to the Mayor of Boston in 1586, warning against any talk being allowed of 'Jesuits and Seminaries' in the inns and ale houses of the town. This letter was signed by two of Elizabeth I's Lord Lieutenants, Sir Anthony Thorold and Sir Edward Dymock (Dymoke). These two families are still prominent in Lincoln-shire's life. The nearest executions were at Lincoln in 1600 when Fathers

Thomas Sprott and Thomas Hunt, two of the Douai priests, were condemned to death for being Catholic priests and were hung, drawn, and quartered on 11th July of that year, and in 1644 when Robert Preece, a Huntingdonshire layman was shot by Puritan soldiers.

But Boston had one glorious representative among the Penal Martyrs. Richard Yaxley was born in Boston. His father owned land at Benington and his mother had come from a Wainfleet family. Richard Yaxley studied at the Douai seminary, although while it was in temporary exile at Reims following difficulties with the French Government. He was ordained in 1585 and came to England early in the following year. Father Yaxley joined an earlier arrival, Father George Nichols, and the two priests worked in and around Oxford, an area where there were still many families loyal to the old religion and, thus, many safe hiding places. Father Yaxley survived for three years before being arrested in an Oxford inn, *The Catherine Wheel*, near the church of Saint Mary Magdalene. Also arrested were Father Nichols, the landlady of the inn, who was a Catholic widow whose name was not recorded, and two laymen, one a Catholic guest at the inn and the second a servant there.

There is space here only to give a brief version of the sufferings of the arrested Catholics. They were questioned by the Vice-Chancellor and several priests from the University. Father Nichols admitted to being a priest in an attempt to save the others but it was soon discovered that Father Yaxley was also a priest. All four men were sent to London where they were tortured and examined again but the four refused to deny their faith. It was decided that they should all die but were returned to Oxford for the formality of a trial. The four men were condemned to death, the two priests to be hung, drawn, and quartered, the laymen to be hung only. The Catholic landlady had her property and goods confiscated and was condemned to life imprisonment.

The execution of the two priests and their colleagues took place in Oxford on 5th July 1589. Father Nichols died first, Father Yaxley next; the two laymen followed. All went bravely to their deaths. The heads of the two priests were severed and their bodies quartered. The pieces were then placed on very high poles at the city gates. Despite the fact that the quartered bodies had been placed in boiling water so that the nerves would not shrink and were now fixed in such a manner that all the hands fell downwards, the right hand of Father Nichols was afterwards found lifted up and raised in the air, stretched out towards the city. Many of the Oxford folk believed the hand was accusing the city of the death of the priests.

Boston's Richard Yaxley was certainly a martyr for his faith but his name is among those whose cause has not yet been considered for canonization or beatification. In the official language of the Church, he is the Venerable Richard Yaxley as are the three comrades executed with him.*

* I must acknowledge the benefit of some detailed notes on Father Yaxley prepared by Father Bernard Grimley when he was parish priest in 1946.

The relentless persecution almost succeeded in killing off the Catholic faith in England. The last priest was executed in 1680; a Jesuit priest died in prison in 1692, and priests could be arrested for saying Mass as late as 1767. Unconfirmed records show that Boston contained only four Catholics in 1709, harassed lay people with no civil rights and forbidden to hold any official employment however humble. There were no Catholic schools nor teachers. In 1767 there were ten Catholics in the town but by 1781 there were none left. The Catholic faith in out-of-the-way Boston had finally died through official persecution and a prolonged absence of priests.

THE FAITH RETURNS

This disappearance of Catholicism from Boston was not destined to last more than fifty years at most – a short period of time in the history of the Church – for two factors were combining to bring about the restoration of the Catholic Church in England. The first of these was the growing spirit of tolerance shown by the Protestant population of England. When the Douai seminary was closed down, following the French Revolution in 1789, there were no objections when this establishment, still financed by the Pope, returned to England in 1793 and took up residence at Old Hall, Ware, in Hertfordshire, to become Saint Edmund's College, and at Crook Hall, County Durham, this part later moving to nearby Ushaw. The Jesuits had also hung on with determination to their links with England and various Jesuit 'missions' started to appear. It is probable that Lincoln was the nearest place to Boston with any substantial Catholic following and there were probably Jesuit priests there, unofficially but tolerated, by the early 1800s.

But the main impetus given to the relaxation of the persecution of Catholics undoubtably came from Ireland. The Reformation had not succeeded in Ireland, the Protestant cause making little progress outside those centres where the British Army and civil government were based. The priest hunts had never been so effective in Ireland and the Catholic faith had never been extinguished there; 80 per cent of the population had probably remained Catholic. The whole of Ireland was still then part of the United Kingdom and it was now deemed intolerable that so many of its citizens should be denied the vote and refused entry to official positions because they were Catholics.

Pressure from the Irish and the more tolerant outlook in England finally brought the Catholic Relief Act – often known as the Catholic Emancipation Act – into law in 1829. The relief was limited at first but welcome. Catholic bishops were restricted in their activities; all priests had to register with the authorities; the Jesuits were not supposed to recruit new members to their order; priests could not assist at marriages; Catholic schools could not yet be established. But it was no longer illegal to be a Catholic priest, to baptize babies and converts, to say or hear Mass.

Fig 1. Saint Mary's about 1930 : the Presbytery can be seen to the left with a garden in front.

Fig 2.   *Fig* 3.

Two views of Saint Mary's in September 1977. Showing the modern car parking space replacing the garden (*see page* 36) and the new porch and extension (*see page* 40).

15

Fig 4. The fine stone altar installed by Father Croft which remained for about 90 years until replaced by the altar shown below (*see page* 36).

Fig 5. The marble altar installed by Father O'Brien but soon to be replaced by the altar shown opposite because of changes in the Liturgy of the Mass.

Fig 6. Interior of Saint Mary's today

Fig 7. The present altar, at which the priest faces the congregation, installed by Father McLaughlin (*see page* 39).

Fig 8. The side altar today, dedicated to Saint Mary the Mother of God.

Fig 9. Interior of Saint Mary's from the altar steps today, showing the choir
gallery installed by Father Scott (*see page* 21).

SAINT MARY'S PARISH

THE NEW CHURCH

Just as it had been pressure from Ireland that had helped to bring about the recent relaxation of the legal restrictions against the English Catholics, so it was the actual movement to England of large numbers of Irishmen that provided the basis for many of the Catholic parishes being re-established in the early 1800s. There was a particular reason why the Boston area should have become the home for so many of these Irishmen. In 1809 and 1818 two Acts of Parliament had set in motion further extensive work of draining the Fens. At this time before the large-scale use of mechanical excavators, there was work here for thousands of labourers and it was Ireland – overpopulated and underdeveloped – who provided the willing manpower. Two sources say that the Irish who came to this area were drawn mainly from County Mayo and it is certain that many Boston Catholics have old roots in this rural area on the exposed west coast of Ireland. So the men of Mayo, and doubtless from other parts of Ireland, came to work around Boston. They dug out many miles of new drainage canals or 'drains' that now keep the farmland of the area fertile and, when agriculture became established on the newly drained land, they formed the backbone of the potato and cereal harvest labour force.

So the pattern was established. Single men came over from Ireland and, at first, would return to their homes at Christmas and for the mid-winter weeks each season. Then 'Paddy' would decide to settle in Boston, either by bringing an Irish girl back with him one year or by marrying a Boston girl. The many children of all these marriages were brought up as Catholics. It did not take long for a sizeable Catholic population to become permanently established in Boston. There is today a narrow lane off Horncastle Road, between Hartley Street and Saint Mary's church, called North Street. It leads to nowhere except the Convent and on to Norprint's Fisher Clark factory. But in the 1810s and 1820s North Street was the place where the Irish settled, in several rows of small cottages. One parishioner says that the whole area between North Street and Norfolk Street was known as 'Irishtown', another even calls it 'The Irish City'.

The Irish brought with them their strong Catholic faith and they needed the ministrations of a priest. It is probable that it was from the Jesuit mission at Lincoln that the first priests came, on short visits at first. The Catholics at Boston were exceedingly fortunate when the Jesuits sent Father Bernard Addis to the town as the first permanent priest. He was truly the father of the reborn Catholic Church in Boston. It should be stated that these were the times before the Irish seminaries started to

19

produce so many priests for England. Father Addis was a Londoner, from an English Catholic family. He had been educated at Stonyhurst public school and he arrived in Boston in 1825, thirty-four years of age and only three years a priest.

When he had entered the Society of Jesus, Father Addis had owned some property. According to the Jesuit custom, he disposed of this and the proceeds of the sale were available when he came to Boston, still without a church or a priest's house. With the permission of his superiors, Father Addis used his money to buy a plot of land on Horncastle Road near the Irish area of housing. He immediately built the Presbytery which still stands today. In this house was the first regular Mass centre in Boston since the Reformation about 300 years earlier. As soon as the house was completed, work commenced on the new brick-built church which is now so familiar to Bostonians. It is probable that most of the work on the church was done in the year 1826 and it was completed and ready for use in 1827.

The Catholics of that period, and the many more who followed in the next 150 years, were very fortunate that Father Addis had both the financial resources and the wisdom and farsightedness to build both the Presbytery and the church of such good quality material and sound construction. The name of the builder and the cost is, unfortunately, not known but both buildings were handed to the Catholics of Boston free of debt and built so well that, whatever financial problems future priests and parishioners may have had, the maintainance of the fabric of both buildings would not be an undue expense.

Basically the church itself and the front part of the Presbytery we know today differs little from Father Addis's creation in 1827 but in minor ways there are many differences. In the church of Father Addis's time there was only a small altar facing the back wall as was the custom until the 1960s, probably no raised sanctuary, and without the existing altar rails. It is possible that there was no seating of any kind for some months and, when the first seats were purchased, they were the low, continental type, rush-covered, individual seats that could be turned round and used as kneelers. There was no gallery, possibly no organ nor piano, no porch, and no outside bell. Lighting was probably provided by oil lamps or candles and there was no central heating. The door from the church into the sacristy and the house was not the one from the sanctuary in current use but was where the side altar now stands. The side altar was not to be built for 120 years. The ground between the Presbytery and Horncastle Road was a garden. There was no convent and no school. The new church in 1827 was almost at the edge of the town at that time. Most of Horncastle Road, past the junction with Norfolk Street, was open country and the few houses in Willoughby Road, the other side of the Maud Foster Drain, were in the parish of Skirbeck. The manner in which this first church and house were extended and altered in following years will be described in subsequent passages of this book.

20

So the new Catholic parish of Saint Mary was established in Boston through the strange combination of an intellectual, ascetic English Jesuit priest and a host of Irish-born labouring men and their families.

Father Addis did not remain long with the new parish. His superiors moved him on three years after the church was completed. He worked for many more years in many more parishes and, later, as librarian in some of the Jesuit houses. He died in 1879, in a Jesuit house at Roehampton, aged eighty-nine years. Few priests are fortunate enough to build a new church and, although his stay in Boston had been a short one, it is known that Father Addis never forgot his achievement here. His obituary in *The Tablet* of Oct. 11th 1879 says, 'It was indeed a happy day for him when he saw the temple which he had raised to the honour of God filled with a congregation of grateful Catholics who had long prayed for this blessing. The memory of that day never passed away – it was a consolation to him to the end.'

THE YEARS OF THE JESUIT MISSION

There was as yet no proper diocesan organization and Boston was due to remain a Jesuit mission for another thirty years. Father Addis was followed by Father Jenkins, Father Joseph Postelwhite, and Father Charles Lomax.* Nothing of interest is known about the eleven years that these three priests spent here. It was presumably a time of consolidation and no major changes took place.

Most impact was made by the next Jesuit, Father John Scott, who came in December 1839 and was destined to be here for the next fifteen years. It is recorded that Father Scott was much respected by all classes in Boston during these years.† He was probably on good terms with the priests at the Stump because a very sound 120 years-old choir gallery, removed from the Stump during restoration work in 1851, was moved to Saint Mary's and re-erected at the back of the church. It is not recorded whether this was a gift or whether it had to be paid for but it became a useful part of Saint Mary's and is still standing, having served 270 years in these two Christian churches.

In the last years of his fifteen-year stay, Father Scott became sick and infirm. The Jesuits sent a succession of assistant priests to help him but, unfortunately, the names of these have not survived. During Father Scott's final illness, his nephew Father John Rigby was the assistant and it was he who had the sad task of officiating at Father Scott's funeral in December 1854. Father Scott, the first of only three priests to die while

---

* A full list of parish priests appears at the end of this booklet.

† Many of the details of this period and of the next fifty years are taken from a pamphlet produced in 1899 to advertise a four-day Bazaar and Fancy Fair held in Saint Mary's School. The introduction to this pamphlet gives a 'potted history' of the parish to that year. I am much indebted to the unknown author of this work.

at work in the parish, was buried just outside the church alongside the footpath of Horncastle Road. His gravestone is still there.

Father Rigby was only destined to remain four more years but his stay was a most important one. It was he who decided that a school should be built for the Catholic children of Boston. He spent his years trying to raise enough money for this. The first school, when it was built, was no more than a single classroom built onto the back wall of the church; it is the room that is now reached up a short flight of stairs from one of the newer classrooms. The exact date of its erection is not known but it unlikely that Father Rigby stayed long enough to see its completion.

When Father Rigby left in 1858, the Jesuit mission in Boston came to an end. St. Mary's church was now thirty-one years old and the good Jesuits had provided the first five parish priests. Our thanks are due to the memory of Father Addis and his comrades for their fine work during what must have been the difficult, though probably exhilerating, years of the return of Catholicism to Boston.

THE DIOCESE TAKES OVER

Although the Catholic Emancipation Act had been passed in 1829, no new Catholic diocesan organization was created for nearly twenty years. At first the church in England was divided into a number of 'districts'; Lincolnshire was in what was called the Midland District and later the Central District under Bishop Walsh in Birmingham. It was not until 1847 that a proper Catholic Hierarchy was re-established in England.

Lincolnshire now came under the diocese of Nottingham; this was a new partnership because the two counties had never been in the same diocese before the Reformation. Saint Barnabas church in Nottingham, built fourteen years after Saint Mary's at Boston, became the Cathedral. So hard up for suitably experienced priests was the Catholic Church in England that Bishop Hendron, the first Bishop of Nottingham, was already aged sixty years and a sick man when appointed. He had time to do little more than incorporate the twenty-eight mission parishes of five counties into the new diocese and to meet the mere thirty-one priests who served them before he resigned two years later.

Bishop Richard Roskell, the next bishop, was a younger and more vigorous man and was able to establish a diocesan structure more soundly. By 1854 he could spare one of his priests for Boston and so relieve the Jesuits from their mission. Father A. Chépy was a French priest, one of many Continental priests loaned to the new English Church. He served in Boston for eleven years before being released to return to France in 1865. The next seventeen years saw five more diocesan priests – Father (later Canon) William Croft, Father J. T. Hoeben, Father Herman

Sabela, Father Peter Sabela, and Father Richard O'Halloran. Father Hoeben was probably Belgian and the two Sabelas certainly were. They were brothers and Herman Sabela actually had two spells in Boston.

These first twenty-eight years of the diocesan priests appear to have been quiet ones. On a visitation to the district by a new bishop, Bishop Bagshawe, in 1878, there were found to be 304 Catholics in Boston and Skirbeck, with 167 Easter duties* being recorded. It is unfortunate that there is no record of any parish numbers before that year so that its growth cannot be measured, but Boston was certainly much stronger in Catholics than other towns nearby. Bishop Bagshawe's visitation found that Sleaford, Spilsby, Skegness, and Wainfleet had only twenty Catholics between them. The Irish influence was still very strong and had probably been reinforced by the great potato famines between 1845 and 1849 but a steady process of anglicization was also taking place. The children and grandchildren of the original Irish never knew any other home than England and were all the time marrying into English families. There was too a steady stream of converts drawn to this new church and religion in Horncastle Road. My own great-grandparents became Catholics at some time during this period after being attracted by the singing at Benediction heard through the open doors of the church one summer evening. This process of change from the original membership of the parish based on the immigrant Irish would be a gradual and continuing one.

Structurally the church did not change as much as the people in these years. Father Croft did build a fine new altar and paid for it from a fund raised mainly from penny-a-week collections from the parishioners. Father Peter Sabela, perhaps to celebrate the first fifty years of the church in 1877, had the interior painted, built a small belfry, put up a set of Stations of the Cross and seven statues – three on the sanctuary and the four apostles to stand on pedestals built into the interior side walls of the main church. The Stations of the Cross were replaced twenty years later but Father Sabela's altar was built so well that it and the seven statues did not disappear until Father O'Brien's drastic modernisation eighty years later.

The school did not change at all. The single room built on to the back of the church was the only classroom for thirty years. The first School Log Book that has survived was started by a new schoolteacher, when she took charge, with these entries.

Sarah Heaney Teacher with Provisional Certificate took charge of this school March 8th 1875.

---

* For the non-Catholic the term 'Easter duty' may be strange. It is an obligation for Catholics to attend confession and receive communion at Eastertide. A count is made of the number of confessions heard between Ash Wednesday and Trinity Sunday and this figure is sent to the diocese as an annual census return of "Easter Duties".

Apparatus for carrying on the school work was as follows :—

1 dozen   Burns Standard III
1   ,,   Third Book of lessons
½   ,,   Burns Standard II
½   ,,   ,,   Primer
1   ,,   Arithmetic books
2½   ,,   copybooks
½   ,,   Sullivans Grammar
½   ,,   ,,   spelling book superseder
3 Mavor's spelling books

Maps of England, France, Spain, Italy, Scotland, North Germany, South Germany, Central Europe, India, North America, United States, Eastern Hemisphere, Australia, Africa.

Number of children present at the first meeting was sixteen.

Commenced classrolls (Standard Register).

Examined children and classified them according to the standards of the Revised Code.

Drew up a Time Table.

A record of the report of Her Majesty's Inspector, following his visit on 28th June 1877, reads:

The attentance (sic) at this School seems to be very bad. The four children who had kept their times did pretty well in standert (sic) work. Of the Infants three Boys did fairly, the others knew next to nothing. The singing is pretty good, but the needlework is of very poor quality. Improvement will be looked for next year. No Grant can be recommended under Article ig (C). A proper supply of Reading Books and Cards is wanted.

Already, little more than two years after Miss Heaney had taken charge, another teacher, Mary O'Donnell, had come and gone and Catherine Quirke was now in charge. The turnover in teachers was rapid – Annie Massam, Sarah Kelly, Christina Hutchinson, Kate Rose Joyce, Annie Coulehan – many of them probably Irish girls who were on their way to the altar soon after taking up their posts.

CANON O'DONAGHUE AND FATHER GATTIE

By 1882 the parish was fifty-five years old and had been cared for by twelve priests. But the next fifty-three years were to see only two parish priests – Father (later Canon) P. J. O'Donaghue from 1882 to 1913 and Father Joseph Gattie from 1913 to 1935. These two long-serving priests represent the arrival of the period within living memory for there are a few people in the parish who can remember Canon O'Donaghue and many who remember Father Gattie. The two priests could hardly have been more different in character and manner and in their effect upon the parish they served.

24

Father O'Donaghue came to Boston from Lincoln. He must have already known something about his new parish because at Lincoln he had been curate to Canon Croft, the priest at Boston until eleven years earlier. Father O'Donaghue has been described as 'a tall, austere, reserved man, as Irish as Irish can be. He never said anything humorous in the pulpit.' Another parishioner remembers him as 'a tall, white-faced, white-haired gentleman, a bit on the strict side,' He was sometimes accused of showing favouritism towards anyone with an Irish surname and his influence with the Irish was certainly immense. The police often sent for him when there was trouble in the Irish cottages in North Street 'Father O'Danaghue soon quietened them down.' He was certainly an able administrator of the parish's affairs and was sufficiently well thought of to be elected to the Boston School Board for several years despite much opposition; he did indeed top the poll – a far cry now from the days at the begining of the century when Catholics could not even vote, let alone hold public office.

Father O'Donaghue's reign of more than thirty years saw many improvements to the parish. He started off in his first year with a new central heating system – the pipes of which are probable the same ones that are in the church today. In 1884 he built two more classrooms, costing £400; they were built on to the existing room and are on the left-hand side as one walks down the playground today. In his next series of improvements Father O'Donaghue was much helped by some very generous benefactors; perhaps he had a very persuasive manner. Miss Frances Smith gave £200 for the purchase of a second-hand organ from the Stump in 1885 and the same lady, together with her sister and brother, gave £900 for the purchase of four cottages on Horncastle Road and the land behind. Frances Smith then gave the £800 necessary to build on this land the fine new Convent of Saint Paul which still stands in its original form. Early in 1886 the first three nuns of the Sisters of Charity of Saint Paul arrived, probably from their mother convent at Selly Park, Birmingham, and they took over the reponsibility for the school and its sixty pupils at that time. So successful were the nuns and so great the demand for places that a new infants school of two classrooms was built (at the Norfolk Street end of the present school) at a cost of £500.

In the spring of the following year, 1888, Father O'Donaghue was off again with a thorough renovation of the church. It was completely redecorated, a new set of benches were bought, the sanctuary was enlarged, new altar rails were erected, and a new porch built. The total cost of all this work was £600 and again Frances Smith and her sister helped with the money. Their benches and altar rail still serve in the church. The existing pulpit was also erected at this time, the expense being borne by a Grantham lady, Mrs. Ford. It was built in 1891 but the inscription on it commemorates George Whitworth who had died five years earlier.

In 1895 the school needed expanding yet again and one more classroom was added. This was probably the upstairs room above the block which now joins the two wings of Saint Mary's School. The cost of this was £450 and the building work was carried out in the summer holidays. The school had thus increased in size from one classroom to six in just twelve years. Its capacity was 300 pupils at a density far higher than would be allowed today. The last recorded improvement carried out by Father O'Donaghue was the purchase, in 1899, of the present-day Stations of the Cross. These came from Meyer and Company of Munich.

It is possible to give more details of life in the school at this time. Before the nuns had come there had obviously been great difficulty in obtaining and retaining good teachers. The School Log Book entries for October-November 1885 reveal what must have been a chaotic situation. Miss Joanna Prendergast took charge of the school in October and her entries in the log for the next six weeks show a daily record of trouble with the children and their parents on the one hand and with the parish priest on the other. She tried to introduce homework, which the parents resisted; she could not get the children to bring the weekly payment of fees that was obviously demanded at that time; she was very free with the cane, which led to some of the boys who had been punished refusing to come back to school. Father O'Donaghue was clearly determined to keep Miss Prendergast in order. He told her off for taking part in political activities, and, finally, on his return from a holiday in Ireland, he dismissed her. He then took her Log Book and, at the end of her long catalogue of conflict, noted pithily in red ink:

The paras in the foregoing report, marked with Nos 1, 2, 3, 4, 5, 6, 7, 8, 9, 10, 11, 12 and 13 in the margin are entirely false.

P. J. O'Donaghue
Manager

The replacement head teacher was Miss Frances Smith, the lady who was giving so much money to the parish at that time.

The nuns had taken over the school soon after this. They were nearly all Irish and a new order of school life was definitely established with the nuns offering a more devoted and settled standard of teaching than that of the barely-trained girls who had come and gone so frequently in the first quarter of a century of the school's life. Some of the elementary schools in Boston refused to take the poorest children of the town but the charitable nuns turned no one away and the poor often finished up at Saint Mary's whether they were Catholic or not. Regular visits are recorded of speakers whose subjects were 'hygiene' and 'temperance'. The nuns also ran a small private school for the children of better-off families in the convent for some years and even took in boarding students, but this private school had closed by 1914. At the other extreme, one much-loved nun, Sister Theresa, also ran an evening class for illiterate adults for several years.

Father O'Donaghue's whirlwind of improvement seemed to have run its course by the turn of the century and little more was done in his last

Fig 11. Father Leo Bermingham

Fig 10. Father Gattie with Mayor Curley of Boston, U.S.A. 22nd May, 1931.

Fig 12. Monsignor Bigland presenting the Benemerenti medal to Miss E. A. Swain

Fig 13. Father Terence Nunn and Miss 'Cissie' Ketterer with Saint Mary's scouts and cubs about 1942. (The author is second from the right in the front row.)

Fig 14. Doctor Bernard Grimley

Fig 15. Father Christopher O'Brien

Fig 16. Father Neil McLaughlin with a group of parishioners

Fig 17. Father Daniel Clavin

Fig 18. Father Daniel Reid

Fig 19. The Nuns in Saint Paul's convent in the 1920's
Sr. Philomena, Sr. Joseph, Sr. Chantelle, Sr. Winifred, Sr. Gerard
Sr. Isobel (choirmaster) Sr Theresa, Mother Rose.

Fig 20. Father Bermingham saying Benediction in the convent garden.

Fig 21. The convent today. Sister Hilda and Sister Sabina, the only nuns now in the
convent, are in the porch.

thirteen years in Boston; perhaps he felt that he could relax a little after his earlier efforts. He continued to preside over the parish in his stern but efficient manner during this quieter period. The years of rapid expansion were over for the time being. The Catholic population of Boston was almost static, being numbered at 326 in 1881 and 341 in 1901. With old age and failing health, Canon O'Donaghue was allowed to leave in 1913 and he retired to Grimsby where he died a few years later. He had served thirty-two years at Saint Mary's, far more than any other priest in the history of the parish.

Father O'Donaghue's successor was of a completely different character. Father Joseph Gattie was a Belgian priest sent to help the diocese in its seemingly never-ending shortage of priests. His real name was Joseph M. Edmund de Hoult but he had apparently adopted the simpler name of 'Gattie'. It was an action typical of the man. He was a small, gentle, unassuming, unassertive priest but very devout and loving of people. He was poor, with no knowledge of the English financial system and apparently no desire to acquire such a knowledge. His time in Boston was one long financial crisis yet he refused ever to ask for money from the pulpit and was content that God would guide him in his poverty. His clothes were always very shabby except for one incongruous outfit of top hat, frock coat, and gaiters which someone in Belgium had once told him that the English always wore on formal occasions and which he could be seen wearing on such occasions. He was very generous to the poor families of the parish and could often be seen trudging off to visit one of them with a parcel under his arm. His main relaxation was the tending of the grape vines that he planted in a large glasshouse in the garden behind the Presbytery. No more need be said about the character of Father Gattie than that he was loved by every member of his parish.

Within a year of his arrival in Boston the First World War broke out and many of the men of the parish went off to fight. Father Gattie was soon having to perform the sad duty of announcing the death of one of his congregation and of leading the saying of the *De Profundis* for his soul. The first to die was Private W. M. McGuire of the 4th East Surreys who died of wounds on 19th May 1915. Eight men in all were to die before the war ended in 1918 – six soldiers, one sailor at the Battle of Jutland, and one airman who died of illness.

Although Father Gattie stayed twenty-two years in Boston, there is not much more that can be said about his time here. As far as is know, not one major building project or improvement was carried out during this time. This is partly because Father Gattie had inherited all of Canon O'Donaghue's improvements, partly because he never had any money to spare for his own works. In the later years of his time in Boston, Father Gattie's financial difficulties became so great that a body of parishioners was formed and this took over from him the financial affairs of the parish. This committee was elected by the parishioners and it is probably the only time that Saint Mary's ever had an elected parish council.

By 1933 Father Gattie's health began to fail and for a few months he had the help of a young assistant priest, Father Michael Kelly. Father Gattie died on 12th January 1935. At his funeral his coffin was carried by the men of the parish all the way from the church down Horncastle Road for burial in the old Catholic plot of the public cemetery.There was an unusual sequel to Father Gatties' death. The next priest to come to St. Mary's found Father Gattie's chalice and sent it to a young friend elsewhere in the diocese who had just been ordained. This new priest, Father Christopher O'Brien, came to Boston as parish priest fifteen years later and gave the chalice to the convent for use in their chapel. It is still there.

MODERN TIMES

Forty-two years have passed since Father Gattie died, years of great change in many aspects of life and certainly in the outward form of the practice of the Catholic religion. These years have also seen a more rapid coming and going of the priests of Saint Mary's. Nine parish priests and at least five curates occupy these forty-two years. If the description of the stay of some of them is only brief, that is because their presence here was also brief.

Father Gattie's replacement was Father Arthur Bird, a priest who at that time was being sent by the bishop to several parishes in turn and not being allowed to settle at any. He was small in stature and sometimes known as 'Dickie Bird'. He was once heard to say that he liked the Boston people well enough but not the Presbytery which was far too cold. But he was a good priest; one parishioner remembers the very devout way in which he said the Stations of the Cross. Father Bird remained in Boston for only seventeen months before being moved on again. He is the senior surviving priest of this parish and is now the Right Reverend Monsignor Canon Bird of the Holy Cross parish in Whitwick, Leicestershire.

The next priest was Father E. Clark but he was only a temporary replacement, filling in the few months before Father Leo Bermingham arrived in October 1936. The only memory that can be found of Father Bermingham was that he was 'a big, fat, boisterous man' who was thought to talk too much politics. Father Bermingham was only here fourteen months before being moved on to Glossop.

Father Bermingham's replacement was to have a ten-year stay. He was the elderly, genial, and charming Monsignor John Bigland, sent to this parish after many years of work in India where he had served as secretary to the Archbishop of Bombay. He was a very English priest, a convert in earlier life after spending some time as a professional actor; his sermons and bearing reflected that earlier occupation. He was very patriotic and had a flagpole erected outside the church at which the Union Jack was flown on national holidays and the Papal flag on church ones. Within a year of his arrival Monsignor Bigland was provided with a young curate, Father Terence Nunn, a popular priest for whom the young people of the parish would have done anything. These two English priests ran the parish efficiently for the next six years.

A new war came, quietly at first, but in May 1940 news came that Pilot Officer Peter Peace had been killed when his aircraft had been shot down by a German fighter during the invasion of France. Peter Peace had been the popular son of Mrs. Peace, the long-serving teacher of the infants class at Saint Mary's School. His death, coming so soon after the opening of serious fighting in France, came as a great shock. At least three more parishioners died in the following war years: Private Anthony Marklew of the 6th Lincolns in Tunisia, Private Richard Appleby of the King's Own Yorkshire Light Infantry in Italy, and Flying Officer Theodore Archard when his Lancaster bomber was shot down one night over France. Unlike the First World War, no memorial to these men has been erected in the church. A belated attempt to produce one in the late 1960s failed. Too much time had elapsed; only three people offered money and there was some confusion over the drawing up of a reliable list of the dead parishioners.

The war years were, however, very active ones for the parish. There was much voluntary war work to be done and various societies flourished. At that period there were strong branches of the Catholic Women's Guild, the Legion of Mary, the Knights of Saint Columba, Girl Guides, Boy Scouts, and Cubs. Saint Mary's School hit the headlines in 1943 when, in a 'Wings for Victory Week' savings campaign, it easily headed the table of results for Boston school savings groups. St Mary's had been allotted a savings certificate sales target of £500 but the school, under the vigorous encouragement of the Head Teacher, Sister Hilda, and with the support of the adults in the parish, raised £3,314. This easily beat the next placed school, the much bigger High School, which raised £2,414. Some of the best school results were mentioned on the national radio but not Saint Mary's. Father Nunn conducted a prolonged correspondence with the local press over this omission but without success. Boston was bombed several times, but not badly and none of the parish's property was damaged. The schoolchildren had to spend some hours in the air-raid shelters during daylight raids. We sang hymns. It was deemed impracticable to provide an effective blackout system for the church and, for six years, there were no evening services during the winter months. Benediction and Stations of the Cross were celebrated in mid-afternoon; this was, of course, before the days of evening Mass.

Monsignor Bigland lived long enough to see peace return in 1945. He had often said that he wanted to die and be buried in Boston but his wish was not granted. He left in September 1945 and died shortly afterwards. Father Nunn had left a few months earlier being replaced by a newly ordained curate, Father Peter McDonagh from Mansfield, whose brother was a professional footballer playing for Boston United. Unfortunately Father Nunn died only a few years later while serving as parish priest at Grantham. Father McDonagh is now parish priest at Melton Mowbray.

The next priest was, like Monsignor Bigland, a man who already had much experience and for whom Boston was to be his last parish. Father Bernard Grimley, Doctor of Divinity, Doctor of Philosophy, was a man with a brilliant mind but troubled by ill health. For many years he had been editor of the *Catholic Times* and many thought, (including Father Grimley himself, says one priest who knew him well), that he would have become a bishop if better health had been granted to him. But Father Grimley suffered from diabetes and from arthritis so acute that he was grossly overweight and every movement caused him difficulty and pain. Perhaps his poor health was also the cause of a very irascible temper.

Father Grimley was a marvellous preacher and, because he could not stand for any length of time, he would deliver his sermons from a dining-room chair placed before the altar. When he had wheezed himself to this, settled down and regained his breath., he would deliver a prolonged but brilliantly phrased extempore discourse on whatever subject he had chosen for that day – often a tirade against the Communists who were at that time persecuting the Church in Eastern Europe, or the politicians and economists of the day who were, according to him, ruining England.

Father Grimley could hardly look after this large parish without assistance and he usually had a curate. The first three were not here for long. The first was Father Gerard Kelly, the second was Father Jeremy Buttimer, a charming Irish missionary on a prolonged holiday from China; he died soon after returning there. The third was Father Leo Lee who also died soon after leaving Boston. But the curate who had to serve Father Grimley for most of this period was Father Francis Bergin, an extremely shy and inexperienced Irish priest – a 'raw recruit' according to one parishioner – who suffered considerably from his parish priest's temper and who could not have enjoyed his two years here.

Despite his health Father Grimley still possessed remarkable willpower and his hard-driving methods stirred up parish life. He had much in common with Canon O'Donaghue and he caused more work to be done in the parish than had been done in the past thirty years since Canon O'Donaghue had left. The cold Presbytery that Father Bird had found so uncomfortable was renovated and its ground floor extended to the rear. A parish hall was purchased; it was an old war-time Fire Service hut from Rosegarth Street. This was re-erected on a site behind the school now occupied by a more modern hall. In the church Father Grimley built the new side altar which stands today and he dedicated it to the memory of Father Addis who had built the original church 120 years earlier. All this work and many more minor projects were ruthlessly pushed through in the immediate post-war years when building materials were so scarce. Money was almost of no importance – 'build first and God and my hard-working parishioners will find the money afterwards' might well have been his motto. Parish fund-raising efforts went on all through the year. The willing were worked very hard; the lazy attempted to keep well out of his way.

There were several interesting events in the church during this period. On 3rd October 1946 Bishop Edward Ellis came from Nottingham and formally consecrated the church. It is not known why this had not been done before. The normal reason preventing this – the presence of a debt on a church – was not valid; Father Addis had built the church without incurring a debt and there had been only minor and temporary periods of indebtedness since then. One innovation by Doctor Grimley was the participation of the congregation in the responses to the mass, a great novelty at that time. Father Grimley was really able to put Boston on the map in March 1950 when the B.B.C.'s Sunday Morning 'People's Service' was broadcast from Saint Mary's for four consecutive weeks.

This was almost Father Grimley's last success. Six months later he was dead of a heart attack. He is only the third parish priest to have died while in Boston and like his two predecessors he is buried here. His body lies in the new Catholic plot of the public cemetery. He had spent only five years at Saint Mary's but his impact during those years had been considerable.

THE LAST TWENTY-SEVEN YEARS

With the year 1950 we reach the final phase of the parish's history up to this 150th Anniversary. The last four priests were all men in the prime of their lives when they came to Boston. They have had to minister to an ever growing parish without any assistant priests; they have had to cope with radical changes in the liturgy, with the turmoil of rapidly changing attitudes in society, and with every increasing financial burdens. Their task has not been easy.

Father Christopher O'Brien arrived after the death of Father Grimley. He had followed Father Grimley into a Leicester parish and now he was following him to Boston. He hoped that he was not destined to follow him down Horncastle Road to the cemetery. Father O'Brien was another Englishman, brought up in Market Harborough, a brisk, intelligent, affable, efficient priest of modern times. He liked fast motor cars and golf, was often about town, and became very popular with many non-Catholics. But he was also a diligent pastor and an able administrator. He had one fault; he was an incorrigibly bad timekeeper. Lucky the parishioner who went to Mass or Benediction and found that the service started before five minutes past the appointed time. Father O'Brien was well aware of his fault but just could not seem to cure it. Just as I shall always remember Father Grimley's sermons, so I shall remember the inevitable delay of several minutes before Father O'Brien came onto the altar.

Father O'Brien was here for the long spell of fifteen years. He continued Father Grimley's building works. The old Fire Service hut serving as a parish hall was scrapped and replaced by the larger and more serviceable building of today. The interior of the church was given a completely new, more modern appearance when the stone high altar installed by Father Croft ninety years earlier was replaced by a new marble altar. Father Peter Sabela's seven statues of eighty years earlier also went and were replaced by the smaller wooden carvings seen in the church today. The whole of the church interior was then redecorated in modern style. Outside, the garden in front of the Presbytery finally disappeared and was replaced with the present-day tarmac car park.

All this had to be paid for. The frantic fund-raising events of Father Grimley's day were continued for some years but their results declined. Father O'Brien eventually closed these down and replaced them with one annual Gift Sunday at which the parish was asked to donate a set sum – £300 if memory serves correctly – in exchange for a promise not to be troubled with fund-raising activities for the remainder of the year. The system worked well until Father O'Brien required £2,000 to pay off a debt on the new parish hall. To cope with this an idea was borrowed from Saint Norbert's parish in Spalding.

The Spalding Catholics had been running a weekly 'numbers' lottery for some time and with much success. They called it the 'Have A Go', after a well-known radio programme in which Wilfred Pickles gave away small amounts of money to contestants on his programme. An identical system was tried in Boston. Members of the parish became 'promoters', selling their batch of numbers at one shilling (5 pence now) each to the townspeople. The Have A Go started here in 1953 and was an immediate success. The weekly draw took place each Sunday after Benediction in the upper room of Saint Mary's School. A weekly turnover of £150 was soon achieved and approximately one third of this was kept as profit. The Have A Go was an immense advance on all previous fund-raising efforts and it looked as though all debts would soon be cleared. But disaster appeared to strike only ten weeks after the opening of the scheme. A senior officer of the local police appeared at the Presbytery and informed Father O'Brien that a complaint had been received that Saint Mary's was running an illegal lottery and that the police were very sorry but they had no choice but to ask Father O'Brien to close down the lottery or face prosecution. Technically the lottery did not comply with the law but it was a mean trick by someone in the town. (The Author believes that he knows who was responsible for the complaint to the police and the motive but fear of libel action restrains him from writing more here).

36

All was not lost, however. The same police officer then gave some valuable unofficial advice. If Father O'Brien closed down the Have A Go lottery and started a new one under a new name and with slightly different rules, the police could not see that there would be any objection. The advice was taken and 'Saint Mary's Development Society' replaced Saint Mary's Have A Go Club. It ran for twenty-two years but was always known, unofficially, as the 'Have A Go'. Exact figures are not available but it is probable that a sum of between £20,000 and £30,000 in profit was raised for parish projects. Much credit is due to those organisers and promoters who kept this lottery running for so long after the initial enthusiasm for it had passed.

One pleasant event during the last year of Father O'Brien's time here was the installation, in May 1965, of the first Catholic Mayor of Boston. The very first mayor in 1545, Nicholas Robertson, had once been an Alderman of Saint Mary's Guild but the Reformation had come just before Boston gained the right to have a Mayor and Robertson had, by then, transferred his allegience to the Anglican Church. The new Mayor and Mayoress in 1965 were Councillor Geoffrey and Mrs. Ada Moulder, both very well known in the parish.

By 1965 a development was taking place that was going to require far more money than even the old 'Have A Go' could provide. A new Catholic Secondary Modern School was being built for the parish. Father O'Brien had now been in Boston for fifteen years, the third longest spell of any of Boston's Catholic priests. His health was not as good as it had been and the bishop decided that a younger priest should come and take over. Father O'Brien moved to the smaller parish at Matlock and is still in the diocese, caring for the small parish of Oldcotes in Nottinghamshire. His time in Boston had been a happy and successful one. He said to me recently, 'I loved Boston; it was the best parish I have ever had.'

The young Father Neil McLaughlin came next, from Lincoln. Father O'Brien had been the last of a long run of English priests. His next three successors would all be Irish. Father McLaughlin came from Donegal and Boston was his first parish with the full responsibility of being the parish priest. There is no doubt that he did well here. He was hard-working, efficient, and very popular; his years here were ones of marked progress. Like Father O'Brien he enjoyed a game of golf.

The two major events during these years were connected with each other. The building of the new secondary school was proceeding steadily and it was ready for use at Easter 1967. The credit for the conception of this school should go to Father O'Brien and Bishop Ellis. The story goes back to the early 1960s when there was talk of the old Saint Mary's Primary School being replaced with a new building. Father O'Brien suggested to Bishop Ellis that any new school built should be a combined primary and secondary school. Bishop Ellis accepted the principle of this suggestion but took the idea further by saying that there should be two new schools, the first being a secondary school large enough to cater for the senior children in Boston and for the senior children in Spalding, there being no Catholic school accommodation at all in Spalding for their older children. The idea met with much resistance from the Holland County Council Education Committee – let it be said on financial rather than on religious grounds – although the Director of Education, Sam Newsom, was very sympathetic. After a long and difficult series of negotiations, the Boston Catholics were allowed their legal right and the school was sanctioned. Father O'Brien says that this might never have been achieved without the support of Sam Newsom.

A site was eventually obtained in Tollfield Road and the secondary school was built at a cost of £76,684. There was room for 150 pupils. The formal opening was performed on 10th May 1967 by Bishop Ellis. The new school was dedicated to Saint Bede, the English scholar and monk of Durham. A second Catholic Mayor, Councillor Martin Middlebrook (author of this booklet) was present. Doctor Patrick Donovan was the first Chairman of the Govenors and Mr. John Kilshaw was appointed Headmaster from thirteen applicants.

The new school was a triumph for Boston's Catholics but these Catholics now had to start paying off £43,500 plus interest towards the cost of it. One feels that Father McLaughlin had been sent to Boston to tackle this financial problem. The answer was the introduction of Christian Giving, on the face of it an entirely new method for the parish but really the implementation of the old Catholic rule that each member should contribute to his parish on a regular basis and *according to his means*. The first Christian Giving Campaign was conducted in the spring of 1966. Again a visit was made to Spalding and the methods used in a successful campaign there were copied. These methods had actually been taken from an American Baptist textbook on the subject. A full-scale campaign lasting ten weeks was then mounted in Boston – all done by the men and women of the parish; professional fund-raisers were not employed.

Visitors were trained, a parish supper was held at which the Christian Giving principles were explained by parishioner speakers not by the parish priest, and then every Catholic wage earner was visited and invited to promise or 'pledge' a regular weekly or monthly sum of money according to his own income. A pledge card was then signed by the donor, placed by him in an envelope which was sealed and returned to the priest. The sum promised had not been disclosed to the visitor and it remained a secret between parishioner and priest. A packet of small envelopes was then left in which the parishioner could make his regular contributions. By means of the number on this envelope, the priest could see whether that person's promise was being kept.

This sophisticated and revolutionary method of raising money was resisted at first by many people, but so carefully was the campaign carried out that it became readily accepted by the majority and was a success. The weekly collections, which had previously been running at about £45, jumped to £120 per week. But Christian Giving is a delicate concept that requires careful attention and regular renewals. Two such renewals of the campaign took place in 1969 and 1972 while Father McLaughlin was still here. A further renewal was planned, after a change of parish priests, for 1974 but, because of an extended coal-miners' strike and a three-day working week in many industries, it was decided to delay this for one year. Again the parish priest changed and there has been no further action since that time.

The original introduction of Christian Giving and the consequent settlement of much of the Saint Bede's debt was Father McLaughlin's greatest achievement here. There were a few other changes during this period. New rules in the liturgy of the Mass forced Father McLaughlin to remove the almost new High Altar installed by Father O'Brien and replace it with the present altar at which the priest faces the congregation. The old Latin Mass was replaced by an English one with the congregation taking part in many of the responses. The movement of one of the Sunday Masses to an early evening time was much appreciated. Bingo was introduced in the parish hall as a fund-raising venture. This, again, was frowned upon by many people but it proved a valuable source of income and is still a successful social gathering for many local people, though mostly non-Catholic. In the church, the organ for which Miss Frances Smith had paid £200 in 1885 finally deteriorated beyond repair, not surprisingly for it had earlier seen many years of service in the Stump. Now a modern form of raising the necessary money, approximately £700, was employed. One large prize, a new Morris Mini-Car or £500 in cash was offered in a 'clock competition'. The buyer of each ticket was supposed to guess the time at which a clock in a sealed parcel would stop. In fact it was really a thinly disguished lottery which might have been considered illegal at that time with a prize above £100 in value. No one complained to the police on this occasion, however. The money for a new organ was raised almost painlessly and a parishioner, Mrs. Conway of Spilsby Road, won herself £500 in cash.

One of Father McLaughlin's final acts was to recommend the award of the Papal *Benemerenti* medal to Mr. Harry Middlebrook for his services to the parish over many years. As far as is known, this was only the second such award in the parish's history; the first had been to Miss Ethel Swain, a well-known benefactress in the 1930s and 1940s. Harry Middlebrook's medal arrived just in time to be handed over by Father McLaughlin at a Parish Dinner in the Assembly Rooms. Attending that dinner was Father Daniel Clavin, already designated as the next parish priest.

Father Neil McLaughlin left in April 1972 after giving seven valuable years to Boston. His energies and talents were now required for the building up of a new parish in Nottingham.

This little history has nearly reached its conclusion. Father Daniel Clavin came in May 1972 with his cousin, Maureen, as housekeeper. He was from the Irish county of Offaly. Although an experienced priest, all Father Clavin's service had been abroad as a missionary or teaching in an English seminary. Boston was his first experience of parish life and he was quite clearly baffled by the administrative complexities of it. He was a little like Father Gattie – of quiet manner, unassertive, financially unsophisticated, but very devout. Again like Father Gattie, his parishioners took to him readily and they prepared to rally round and help him solve his financial difficulties. Father Clavin was unfortunate enough to come to Boston just at the start of the period of financial inflation with which we are still inflicted, five years later.

The Silver Jubilee of Father Clavin occured soon after his arrival in Boston and this was duly marked by a concelebrated Mass in the church and a reception for members of the parish at Saint Bede's School. It was a successful and enjoyable day.

Another event during that year was the demolition of the old church porch and its replacement by a new extension, This increased the seating capacity of the church by fifty people at a cost of £5,090. This extension was a good example of the way any project now takes so much time for planning and financial development; the planning of this extension had been started by Father O'Brien, two parish priests earlier.

A new 'coadjutor' bishop, Monsignor James McGuiness, came twice during that year – once for Father Clavin's Silver Jubilee and once for a confirmation visitation. During this last visit he presented a surprise Papal Medal to Mr. Noel Bradley another stalwart in parish service. Monsignor McGuiness became full bishop when Bishop Ellis retired in October 1974.

Father Clavin appeared to becoming well settled in Boston, and was certainly mastering the complexities of parish life, when he was suddenly removed in May 1974, only two years after his arrival. Father Clavin and his housekeeper were very disappointed at this, so too were many of his parishioners who would have preferred a longer stay.

The next priest was Father Daniel Reid, another Irishman, from West Meath. He came to Saint Mary's from Long Eaton. The genial Father Reid has been here for more than three years now. By my reckoning he is the twenty-second parish priest of Saint Mary's Boston and it will be his good fortune to celebrate the 150th year of the parish. It is too soon to assess the impact of his tenure of office here and I hope he will excuse me if I leave it to the writer of a later history to sum up his achievements in Boston.

THE FUTURE

And so Saint Mary's attains its 150th Anniversary. The district it now covers must be one of the largest in the diocese, reaching out to cover the country villages up to ten miles away to the north, west, and south, and as far as the sea on the east. Its nominal estimated Catholic population is 1,000 in 1977 but this figure must represent more than the practising members of the parish. There were 358 Easter Duties – 209 female and 147 male – in 1977 and the average Sunday Mass attendance the previous October was 407. In 1976 there were twenty-five baptisms, seven marriages, and thirteen deaths. The convent now has only two nuns, Sister Sabina who retired in 1974 after thirty-nine years of teaching, and Sister Hilda who will retire next year after forty-one years. We thank them both for these years of service. Saint Mary's School now has approximately 160 pupils on its roll and Saint Bede's has about 150, just under half of whom are from the Spalding area in accordance with the original plan of Bishop Ellis. Saint Bede's has two 'houses' one named after Boston's earliest Saint, Botolph, and the second after Richard Yaxley, whom we hope will be recognised as a second saint.

The parish has a branch of the Knight of Saint Columba, and a strong Women's Guild which refuses to be affiliated to any of the official Catholic organisations but does much good work and whose members enjoy themselves at the same time. Noel Bradley and a few loyal members keep the Saint Vincent de Paul Society alive. There are small but active senior and junior branches of the Legion of Mary. There is no youth club, and no scouts nor guides. The Have A Go died a natural death but bingo lives on.

With the greater movement of population in recent years a large proportion of the parish's membership is now ever-changing but always around a core of older-established families. New arrivals from other parts of the country are sometimes surprised and disappointed that there is not more social life and participation; they sometimes mistake the dogged nature of the Lincolnshire Catholic for apathy. They will find that we are as loyal to our parish as any other but in a quieter and more dour fashion. The parish has a few Dutch families, one Chinese family, at least two French-born ladies, two Polish doctors and their wives, and some Asian doctors and nurses from the new Pilgrim Hospital that was opened by Princess Anne earlier this year. Irish accents are still heard outside the church after Sunday Mass. The Boston Catholics live in a town which is now completely tolerant to the practice of our religion, thanks to the good sense and citizenship of Father Addis and his successors and the five or six generations of Catholics who have grown from the Irish labourers of North Street and the English converts.

In completing this booklet I must admit that I have deliberately written it with an eye to the future. I might just be here in 2027 but by then would be aged ninety-five and long past writing if I should survive to that 200th Anniversary. I hope that someone will carry on where I leave off and that this history of Saint Mary's will be updated on that occasion. I leave the historian of 2027 with a few questions which puzzle us in 1977. He or she may be able to provide some of the answers to these questions.

The most important question is, I think, will we be able to have a continuing supply of priests? To the best of my knowledge, this parish has only supplied two priests for the Nottingham Diocese in 150 years – Father Mullany, at the end of the last century, and Father Patrick Halliday earlier in this century – and Father Stewart Simpson for the Westminster Diocese. The last three priests we have had have all come from Ireland. As much as we respect and admire them and are grateful to their country for sending them, many of the English Catholics have longed for English priests but England does not seem to provide the necessary vocations. There is a possible answer, but will the Vatican recognise the true rights of equality for women and will the year 2027 see a woman priest in Boston?

Will the little community of nuns in St Paul's Convent survive? It is unlikely. Will our schools continue to prosper? All appears well at the moment but there is no sign of a replacement for the ageing Saint Mary's Primary School and none likely while inflation continues at its present high level (17 per cent in the current year) and public spending is being curtailed. The future of Saint Bede's – at present a 'Secondary Modern' – is threatened by a Labour Government determined to force Comprehensive Education upon this community. There has been this threat before but one day it may become a reality and Saint Bede's will have to be fitted into a system for which its small size was never designed. Perhaps the Catholic schools may not have so many demands made upon them in the way of pupil numbers. The birth rate in England is falling at the moment. Baptisms at Saint Mary's averaged only twenty-four per year in the last five years compared with thirty-nine, thirty-three and thirty-four in the three previous sets of five years. Will ecumenism – the movement towards the unity of Christian religions – make any real progress? Much has been said in recent years; little has been really achieved. Perhaps we Catholic are partly to blame but the old belief that our Popes have the unbroken succession back to Saint Peter and thus to Jesus Christ is a hard one to shift from. Will God be able to see the Christians of Boston worshipping together in more than token form in 2027? Will the ailing concept of Christian Giving be revived and, if not, how will the parish be financed in fifty years time?

Of one thing I am sure. Because Father Addis built the little church in Horncastle Road so soundly, that church will surely still be standing. I am sure too that the Catholics of Boston, seemingly passive and undemonstrative in their religion though they be, will be there also.

LIST OF PRIESTS*

1825 – 1828	Fr Bernard Addis S.J.
1828 – 1829	Fr G. Jenkins S.J.
1829 – 1837	Fr Joseph Postelwhite S.J.
1837 – 1839	Fr Charles Lomax S.J.
1839 – 1854	Fr John Scott S.J.
– 1854	Unknown assistant priests
1854 – 1858	Fr John Rigby S.J.
1858 – 1865	Fr A. Chépy (French)
1865 – 1871	Fr William Croft
1871 – 1875	Fr Hoeben (Belgian?)
1875 – 1876	Fr Herman J. Sabela (Belgian)
1876 – 1879	Fr Peter J. Sabela (Belgian)
1879 – 1882	Fr Herman J. Sabela (Belgian)
1882	Fr Richard O'Halloran
1882 – 1913	Fr (later Canon) P. J. O'Donaghue
1913 – 1935	Fr Joseph E. Gattie (Joseph M. Edmund de Hoult – Belgian)
1933 – 1935	Fr Michael Kelly (assistant)
1936	Fr E. Clark
1936 – 1937	Fr Leo Bermingham
1938 – 1945	Mgr John Bigland
1939 – 1945	Fr Terence Nunn (assistant)
1944 – 1945	Fr Peter McDonagh (assistant, overlapping with Fr Nunn for short period)
1945 – 1950	Dr Bernard Grimley
1945	Fr Gerard Kelly (assistant)
1945 – 1946	Fr Jeremy Buttimer (assistant)
1947 –	(exact dates unknown) Fr Leo Lee (assistant)
1948 – 1950	Fr Francis Bergin (assistant)
1950 – 1965	Fr Christopher O'Brien
1965 – 1972	Fr Neil McLaughlin
1972 – 1974	Fr Daniel Clavin
1974 –	Fr Daniel Reid

---

* This list is compiled mainly from the signatures in Baptismal, Marriage, and Burial Registers. Some assistant priests do not seem to have performed many of these ceremonies and the dates given below may not always show the full length of their service in Boston.

HISTORY OF BOSTON SERIES

ISSN 0305 2079

" In the now established tradition of quality of the Series "
– *Lincolnshire Life* (of The Puritan Town of Boston)

History of Boston Series – Number One   **out of print**
    The First Stone and other papers

The Early Medieval History of Boston AD 1086 - 1400 (2nd Edn.) by P. Dover   60p.
    (History of Boston Series - Number Two)   (U.S.A. $1.80)

History of Boston Series - Number Three   42p.
    The Boston Farmers Union and other papers   (U.S.A. $1.20)

The Railways of Boston - their origins and development by Neil R. Wright   **out of print**
    (History of Boston Series - Number Four)

The Puritan Town of Boston by Mark Spurrell, and other papers   60p.
    (History of Boston Series - Number Five)   (U.S.A. $1.35)

Methodism in the Town of Boston by William Leary   80p.
    (History of Boston Series - Number Six)   (U.S.A. $2.00)

Boston and the Great Civil War by A. A. Garner   £1.00
    (History of Boston Series - Number Seven)   (U.S.A. $2.50)

Aspects of Nineteenth Century Boston and District   60p.
    (History of Boston Series - Number Eight)   (U.S.A. $1.35)

The Monumental Brasses in Saint Botolph's Church, Boston by Jeremy Wheeldon   33p.
    (History of Boston Series - Number Nine)   (U.S.A. $1.00)

AN ATLAS OF BOSTON by Frank Molyneux and Neil Wright   £4.50
    (History of Boston Series - Number Ten)   (U.S.A. $10.00)

    This Atlas is a fully bound book approx. 12″ x 8½″ and contains 24 maps – 9 reproductions and 15 originals – all with commentaries. It is a major contribution to the Series and of importance to all socio-economic geographers and all historians interested in representing historical change in the geographical idiom.

Boston's Newspapers by Lionel Robinson   £1.00
    (History of Boston Series - Number Eleven)   (U.S.A. $2.10)

Boston at War by Martin Middlebrook   £1.20
    (History of Boston Series – Number Twelve)   (U.S.A. $3.50)

Boston: Politics and the Sea 1652 – 74 by A. A. Garner   £1.20
    (History of Boston Series – Number Thirteen)   (U.S.A. $3.50)

Banking in Boston by S. N. Davis   £1.20
    (History of Boston Series – Number Fourteen)   (U.S.A. $3.50)

All the above publications should be available through any good bookshop or from the History of Boston Project (plus postage). Except for the Atlas they are of uniform size, 8½″x 6¼″. In the event of difficulty they may be obtained from the publisher. Postage should be added at the rate of 12p. per booklet or 45p for the Atlas. No postage in excess of 50p. for any number need be added.

Hall's Map of Boston 1741 (approx 23½″ x 18¼″) suitable for framing is available in black or sepia (£1.00 post free – specify colour).

Chart of the Wash 1693 (a reduced reproduction of which appears in booklet No. XIII facing page 1.) is also available suitable for framing approx. size 14″ x 18″ (£1.00 post free – black only).
    (Both maps supplied together in one map tube £1.75p. post free).

ISBN 0 902662

GUARDIAN PR
(BOSTON) LTD
NELSON WA'
BOSTON · L